Get Fit and Stay Fit!

Men's Exercise Journal

Activinotes

Activinotes

DAILY JOURNALS, PLANNERS, NOTEBOOKS AND OTHER BLANK BOOKS

Copyright 2016

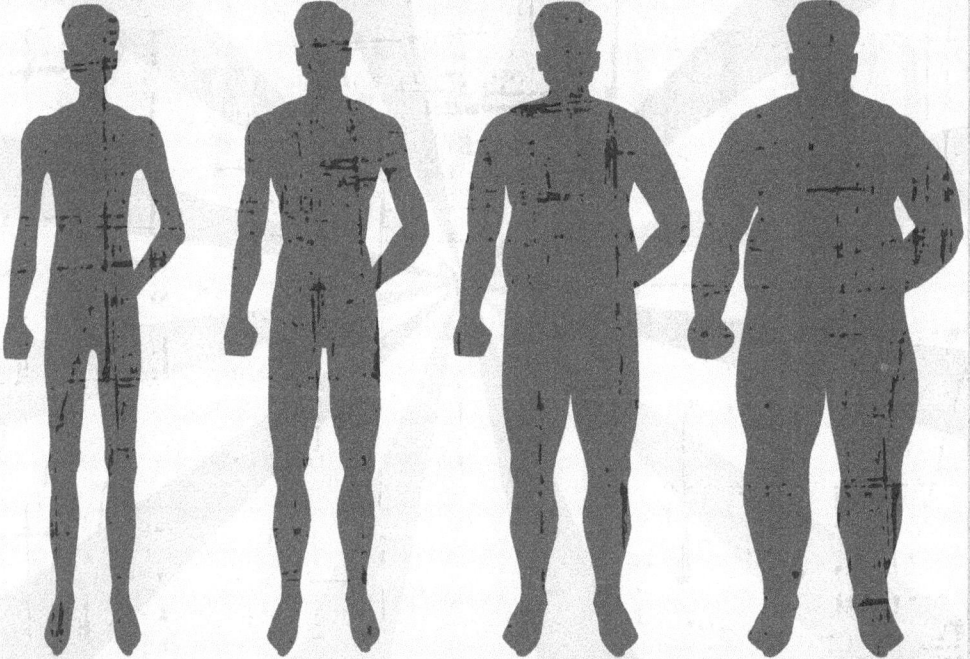

Body Mass Index

Men

Underweight	Healthy weight	Overweight	Obese
<18.5	18.5-24.9	25.0-29.9	>40.0

CALORIES BURNED WITH SPORTS

• • • • • • • • • INFOGRAPHIC

BOXER
Kcal / Hour
800 kcal

BASKETBALL
Kcal / Hour
590 kcal

TENNIS
Kcal / Hour
480 kcal

BADMINTON
Kcal / Hour
550 kcal

JOGGING
Kcal / Hour
750 kcal

88

RUGBY
Kcal / Hour
500 kcal

BASEBALL
Kcal / Hour
350 kcal

FOOTBALL
Kcal / Hour
750 kcal

SWIMMING
Kcal / Hour
700 kcal

_____ Date

	CORE BODY	UPPER BODY	LOWER BODY
EXERCISES			
SETS			
REPS			
WEIGHTS			
REST TIME			

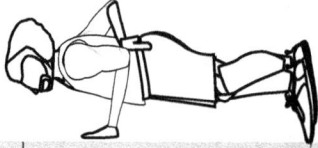

	WARM UP	COOL DOWN
ACTIVITY		
SETS		
REPS		
TIME		
DIST		
INTENSITY		

Notes :

_____
_____
_____
_____
_____
_____

_____ Date

	CORE BODY	UPPER BODY	LOWER BODY
EXERCISES			
SETS			
REPS			
WEIGHTS			
REST TIME			

	WARM UP	COOL DOWN
ACTIVITY		
SETS		
REPS		
TIME		
DIST		
INTENSITY		

Notes :

_____
_____
_____
_____
_____
_____

_____ Date

	CORE BODY	UPPER BODY	LOWER BODY
EXERCISES			
SETS			
REPS			
WEIGHTS			
REST TIME			

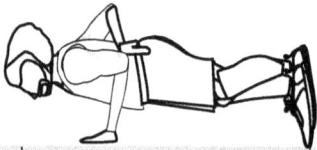

	WARM UP	COOL DOWN
ACTIVITY		
SETS		
REPS		
TIME		
DIST		
INTENSITY		

Notes :

_____
_____
_____
_____
_____
_____

_____ Date

	CORE BODY	UPPER BODY	LOWER BODY
EXERCISES			
SETS			
REPS			
WEIGHTS			
REST TIME			

	WARM UP	COOL DOWN
ACTIVITY		
SETS		
REPS		
TIME		
DIST		
INTENSITY		

Notes :

_____
_____
_____
_____
_____
_____

_____ Date

	CORE BODY	UPPER BODY	LOWER BODY
EXERCISES			
SETS			
REPS			
WEIGHTS			
REST TIME			

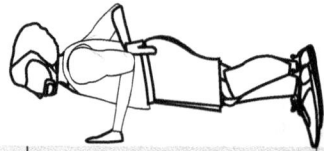

	WARM UP	COOL DOWN
ACTIVITY		
SETS		
REPS		
TIME		
DIST		
INTENSITY		

Notes :

_____
_____
_____
_____
_____
_____

_____ Date

	CORE BODY	**UPPER BODY**	**LOWER BODY**
EXERCISES			
SETS			
REPS			
WEIGHTS			
REST TIME			

	WARM UP	**COOL DOWN**
ACTIVITY		
SETS		
REPS		
TIME		
DIST		
INTENSITY		

Notes :

_____
_____
_____
_____
_____
_____

_____ Date

	CORE BODY	**UPPER BODY**	**LOWER BODY**
EXERCISES			
SETS			
REPS			
WEIGHTS			
REST TIME			

	WARM UP	**COOL DOWN**
ACTIVITY		
SETS		
REPS		
TIME		
DIST		
INTENSITY		

Notes :
_____
_____
_____
_____
_____
_____

_____ Date

	CORE BODY	UPPER BODY	LOWER BODY
EXERCISES			
SETS			
REPS			
WEIGHTS			
REST TIME			

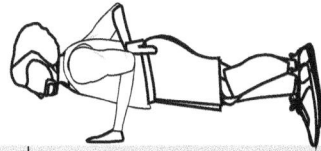

	WARM UP	COOL DOWN
ACTIVITY		
SETS		
REPS		
TIME		
DIST		
INTENSITY		

Notes :

_____
_____
_____
_____
_____
_____

_____ Date

	CORE BODY	**UPPER BODY**	**LOWER BODY**
EXERCISES			
SETS			
REPS			
WEIGHTS			
REST TIME			

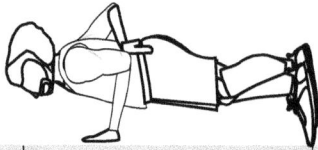

	WARM UP	**COOL DOWN**
ACTIVITY		
SETS		
REPS		
TIME		
DIST		
INTENSITY		

Notes :

_____
_____
_____
_____
_____
_____

_____ Date

	CORE BODY	UPPER BODY	LOWER BODY
EXERCISES			
SETS			
REPS			
WEIGHTS			
REST TIME			

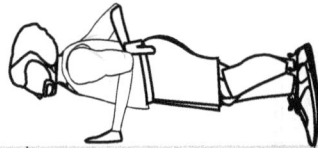

	WARM UP	COOL DOWN
ACTIVITY		
SETS		
REPS		
TIME		
DIST		
INTENSITY		

Notes :

_____
_____
_____
_____
_____
_____

_____ Date

	CORE BODY	UPPER BODY	LOWER BODY
EXERCISES			
SETS			
REPS			
WEIGHTS			
REST TIME			

	WARM UP	COOL DOWN
ACTIVITY		
SETS		
REPS		
TIME		
DIST		
INTENSITY		

Notes :

_____

_____

_____

_____

_____

_____

_____ Date

	CORE BODY	UPPER BODY	LOWER BODY
EXERCISES			
SETS			
REPS			
WEIGHTS			
REST TIME			

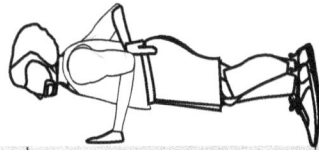

	WARM UP	COOL DOWN
ACTIVITY		
SETS		
REPS		
TIME		
DIST		
INTENSITY		

Notes :

_____
_____
_____
_____
_____
_____

_____ Date

	CORE BODY	UPPER BODY	LOWER BODY
EXERCISES			
SETS			
REPS			
WEIGHTS			
REST TIME			

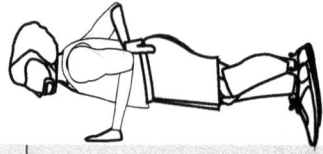

	WARM UP	COOL DOWN
ACTIVITY		
SETS		
REPS		
TIME		
DIST		
INTENSITY		

Notes :

_____

_____

_____

_____

_____

_____

_____ Date

	CORE BODY	UPPER BODY	LOWER BODY
EXERCISES			
SETS			
REPS			
WEIGHTS			
REST TIME			

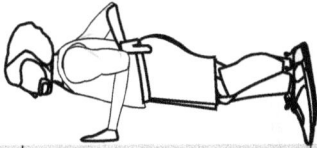

	WARM UP	COOL DOWN
ACTIVITY		
SETS		
REPS		
TIME		
DIST		
INTENSITY		

Notes :

_____
_____
_____
_____
_____
_____

_____ Date

	CORE BODY	**UPPER BODY**	**LOWER BODY**
EXERCISES			
SETS			
REPS			
WEIGHTS			
REST TIME			

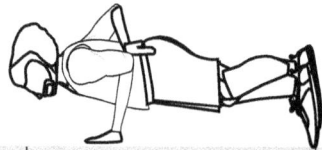

	WARM UP	**COOL DOWN**
ACTIVITY		
SETS		
REPS		
TIME		
DIST		
INTENSITY		

Notes :

_____
_____
_____
_____
_____
_____

_____ Date

	CORE BODY	UPPER BODY	LOWER BODY
EXERCISES			
SETS			
REPS			
WEIGHTS			
REST TIME			

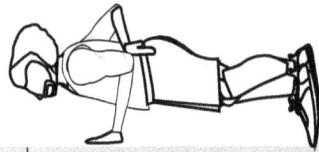

	WARM UP	COOL DOWN
ACTIVITY		
SETS		
REPS		
TIME		
DIST		
INTENSITY		

Notes :

_____
_____
_____
_____
_____
_____

_____ Date

	CORE BODY	**UPPER BODY**	**LOWER BODY**
EXERCISES			
SETS			
REPS			
WEIGHTS			
REST TIME			

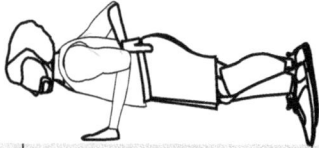

	WARM UP	**COOL DOWN**
ACTIVITY		
SETS		
REPS		
TIME		
DIST		
INTENSITY		

Notes :

_____
_____
_____
_____
_____
_____

_____ Date

	CORE BODY	**UPPER BODY**	**LOWER BODY**
EXERCISES			
SETS			
REPS			
WEIGHTS			
REST TIME			

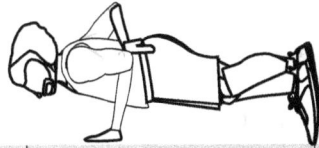

	WARM UP	**COOL DOWN**
ACTIVITY		
SETS		
REPS		
TIME		
DIST		
INTENSITY		

Notes :
_____
_____
_____
_____
_____
_____

_____ Date

	CORE BODY	**UPPER BODY**	**LOWER BODY**
EXERCISES			
SETS			
REPS			
WEIGHTS			
REST TIME			

	WARM UP	**COOL DOWN**
ACTIVITY		
SETS		
REPS		
TIME		
DIST		
INTENSITY		

Notes :
_____
_____
_____
_____
_____
_____

_____ Date

	CORE BODY	UPPER BODY	LOWER BODY
EXERCISES			
SETS			
REPS			
WEIGHTS			
REST TIME			

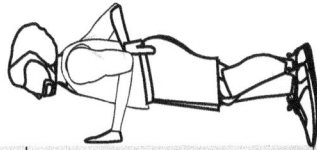

	WARM UP	COOL DOWN
ACTIVITY		
SETS		
REPS		
TIME		
DIST		
INTENSITY		

Notes :

_____
_____
_____
_____
_____
_____

_____ Date

	CORE BODY	**UPPER BODY**	**LOWER BODY**
EXERCISES			
SETS			
REPS			
WEIGHTS			
REST TIME			

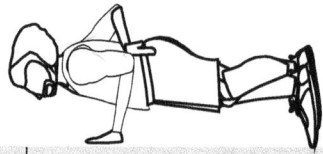

	WARM UP	**COOL DOWN**
ACTIVITY		
SETS		
REPS		
TIME		
DIST		
INTENSITY		

Notes :

_____
_____
_____
_____
_____
_____

_____ Date

	CORE BODY	UPPER BODY	LOWER BODY
EXERCISES			
SETS			
REPS			
WEIGHTS			
REST TIME			

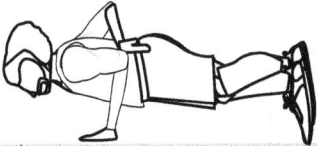

	WARM UP	COOL DOWN
ACTIVITY		
SETS		
REPS		
TIME		
DIST		
INTENSITY		

Notes :

_____
_____
_____
_____
_____
_____

_____ Date

	CORE BODY	UPPER BODY	LOWER BODY
EXERCISES			
SETS			
REPS			
WEIGHTS			
REST TIME			

 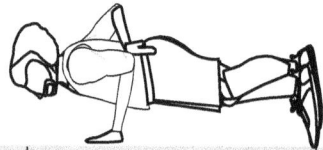

	WARM UP	COOL DOWN
ACTIVITY		
SETS		
REPS		
TIME		
DIST		
INTENSITY		

Notes :

_____
_____
_____
_____
_____
_____

_____ Date

	CORE BODY	UPPER BODY	LOWER BODY
EXERCISES			
SETS			
REPS			
WEIGHTS			
REST TIME			

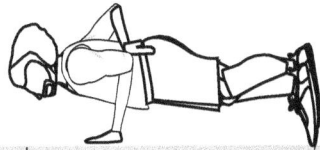

	WARM UP	COOL DOWN
ACTIVITY		
SETS		
REPS		
TIME		
DIST		
INTENSITY		

Notes :

_____
_____
_____
_____
_____
_____

_____ Date

	CORE BODY	**UPPER BODY**	**LOWER BODY**
EXERCISES			
SETS			
REPS			
WEIGHTS			
REST TIME			

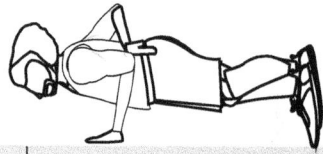

	WARM UP	**COOL DOWN**
ACTIVITY		
SETS		
REPS		
TIME		
DIST		
INTENSITY		

Notes :

_____
_____
_____
_____
_____
_____

_____ Date

	CORE BODY	UPPER BODY	LOWER BODY
EXERCISES			
SETS			
REPS			
WEIGHTS			
REST TIME			

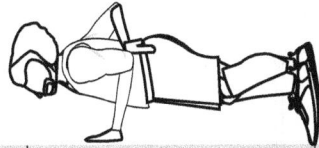

	WARM UP	COOL DOWN
ACTIVITY		
SETS		
REPS		
TIME		
DIST		
INTENSITY		

Notes :

_____
_____
_____
_____
_____
_____

_____ Date

	CORE BODY	**UPPER BODY**	**LOWER BODY**
EXERCISES			
SETS			
REPS			
WEIGHTS			
REST TIME			

	WARM UP	**COOL DOWN**
ACTIVITY		
SETS		
REPS		
TIME		
DIST		
INTENSITY		

Notes :

_____
_____
_____
_____
_____
_____

_____ Date

	CORE BODY	UPPER BODY	LOWER BODY
EXERCISES			
SETS			
REPS			
WEIGHTS			
REST TIME			

	WARM UP	COOL DOWN
ACTIVITY		
SETS		
REPS		
TIME		
DIST		
INTENSITY		

Notes :
_____
_____
_____
_____
_____
_____

_____ Date

	CORE BODY	UPPER BODY	LOWER BODY
EXERCISES			
SETS			
REPS			
WEIGHTS			
REST TIME			

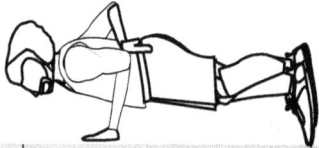

	WARM UP	COOL DOWN
ACTIVITY		
SETS		
REPS		
TIME		
DIST		
INTENSITY		

Notes :

_____

_____

_____

_____

_____

_____

_____ Date

	CORE BODY	UPPER BODY	LOWER BODY
EXERCISES			
SETS			
REPS			
WEIGHTS			
REST TIME			

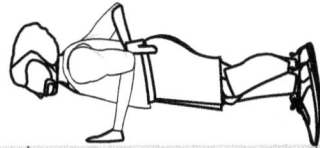

	WARM UP	COOL DOWN
ACTIVITY		
SETS		
REPS		
TIME		
DIST		
INTENSITY		

Notes :

_____
_____
_____
_____
_____
_____

_____ Date

	CORE BODY	UPPER BODY	LOWER BODY
EXERCISES			
SETS			
REPS			
WEIGHTS			
REST TIME			

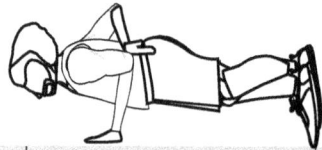

	WARM UP	COOL DOWN
ACTIVITY		
SETS		
REPS		
TIME		
DIST		
INTENSITY		

Notes :

_____
_____
_____
_____
_____
_____

	CORE BODY	UPPER BODY	LOWER BODY
EXERCISES			
SETS			
REPS			
WEIGHTS			
REST TIME			

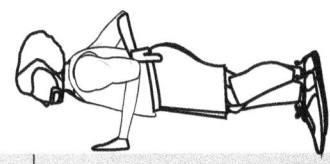

	WARM UP	COOL DOWN
ACTIVITY		
SETS		
REPS		
TIME		
DIST		
INTENSITY		

Notes :

_____
_____
_____
_____
_____
_____

_____ Date

	CORE BODY	UPPER BODY	LOWER BODY
EXERCISES			
SETS			
REPS			
WEIGHTS			
REST TIME			

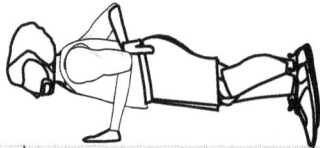

	WARM UP	COOL DOWN
ACTIVITY		
SETS		
REPS		
TIME		
DIST		
INTENSITY		

Notes :

_____
_____
_____
_____
_____
_____

_____ Date

	CORE BODY	UPPER BODY	LOWER BODY
EXERCISES			
SETS			
REPS			
WEIGHTS			
REST TIME			

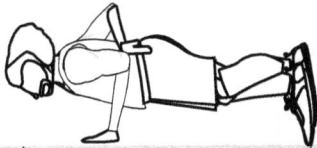

	WARM UP	COOL DOWN
ACTIVITY		
SETS		
REPS		
TIME		
DIST		
INTENSITY		

Notes :

_____
_____
_____
_____
_____
_____

_____ Date

	CORE BODY	UPPER BODY	LOWER BODY
EXERCISES			
SETS			
REPS			
WEIGHTS			
REST TIME			

	WARM UP	COOL DOWN
ACTIVITY		
SETS		
REPS		
TIME		
DIST		
INTENSITY		

Notes :

_____
_____
_____
_____
_____
_____

_____ Date

	CORE BODY	**UPPER BODY**	**LOWER BODY**
EXERCISES			
SETS			
REPS			
WEIGHTS			
REST TIME			

	WARM UP	**COOL DOWN**
ACTIVITY		
SETS		
REPS		
TIME		
DIST		
INTENSITY		

Notes :

_____
_____
_____
_____
_____
_____

_____ Date

	CORE BODY	**UPPER BODY**	**LOWER BODY**
EXERCISES			
SETS			
REPS			
WEIGHTS			
REST TIME			

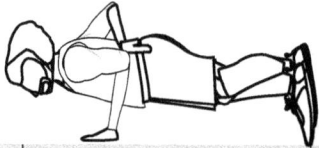

	WARM UP	**COOL DOWN**
ACTIVITY		
SETS		
REPS		
TIME		
DIST		
INTENSITY		

Notes :
_____
_____
_____
_____
_____
_____

_____ Date

	CORE BODY	UPPER BODY	LOWER BODY
EXERCISES			
SETS			
REPS			
WEIGHTS			
REST TIME			

	WARM UP	COOL DOWN
ACTIVITY		
SETS		
REPS		
TIME		
DIST		
INTENSITY		

Notes :

_____
_____
_____
_____
_____
_____

_____ Date

	CORE BODY	UPPER BODY	LOWER BODY
EXERCISES			
SETS			
REPS			
WEIGHTS			
REST TIME			

	WARM UP	COOL DOWN
ACTIVITY		
SETS		
REPS		
TIME		
DIST		
INTENSITY		

Notes :
_____
_____
_____
_____
_____
_____

_____ Date

	CORE BODY	UPPER BODY	LOWER BODY
EXERCISES			
SETS			
REPS			
WEIGHTS			
REST TIME			

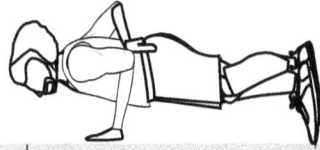

	WARM UP	COOL DOWN
ACTIVITY		
SETS		
REPS		
TIME		
DIST		
INTENSITY		

Notes :
_____
_____
_____
_____
_____
_____

_____ Date

	CORE BODY	UPPER BODY	LOWER BODY
EXERCISES			
SETS			
REPS			
WEIGHTS			
REST TIME			

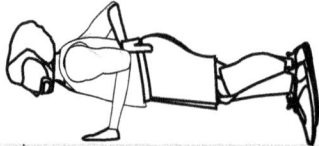

	WARM UP	COOL DOWN
ACTIVITY		
SETS		
REPS		
TIME		
DIST		
INTENSITY		

Notes :

_____

_____

_____

_____

_____

_____

_____ Date

	CORE BODY	UPPER BODY	LOWER BODY
EXERCISES			
SETS			
REPS			
WEIGHTS			
REST TIME			

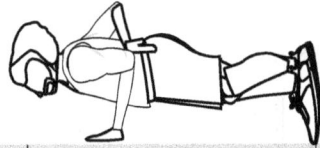

	WARM UP	COOL DOWN
ACTIVITY		
SETS		
REPS		
TIME		
DIST		
INTENSITY		

Notes :
_____
_____
_____
_____
_____
_____

_____ Date

	CORE BODY	UPPER BODY	LOWER BODY
EXERCISES			
SETS			
REPS			
WEIGHTS			
REST TIME			

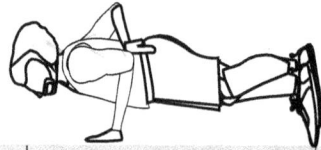

	WARM UP	COOL DOWN
ACTIVITY		
SETS		
REPS		
TIME		
DIST		
INTENSITY		

Notes :
_____
_____
_____
_____
_____
_____

_____ Date

	CORE BODY	UPPER BODY	LOWER BODY
EXERCISES			
SETS			
REPS			
WEIGHTS			
REST TIME			

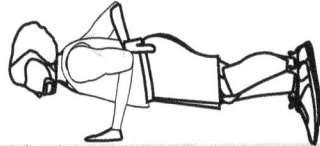

	WARM UP	COOL DOWN
ACTIVITY		
SETS		
REPS		
TIME		
DIST		
INTENSITY		

Notes :

_____
_____
_____
_____
_____
_____

_____ Date

	CORE BODY	UPPER BODY	LOWER BODY
EXERCISES			
SETS			
REPS			
WEIGHTS			
REST TIME			

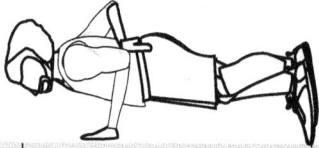

	WARM UP	COOL DOWN
ACTIVITY		
SETS		
REPS		
TIME		
DIST		
INTENSITY		

Notes :

_____

_____

_____

_____

_____

_____

_____ Date

	CORE BODY	**UPPER BODY**	**LOWER BODY**
EXERCISES			
SETS			
REPS			
WEIGHTS			
REST TIME			

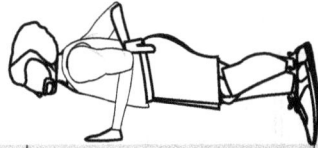

	WARM UP	**COOL DOWN**
ACTIVITY		
SETS		
REPS		
TIME		
DIST		
INTENSITY		

Notes :

_____

_____

_____

_____

_____

_____

_____ Date

	CORE BODY	UPPER BODY	LOWER BODY
EXERCISES			
SETS			
REPS			
WEIGHTS			
REST TIME			

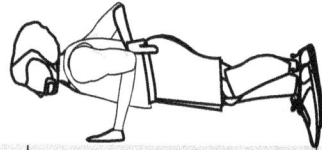

	WARM UP	COOL DOWN
ACTIVITY		
SETS		
REPS		
TIME		
DIST		
INTENSITY		

Notes :

_____
_____
_____
_____
_____
_____

_____ Date

	CORE BODY	UPPER BODY	LOWER BODY
EXERCISES			
SETS			
REPS			
WEIGHTS			
REST TIME			

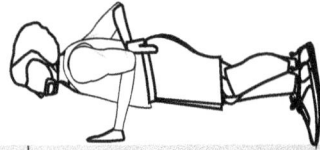

	WARM UP	COOL DOWN
ACTIVITY		
SETS		
REPS		
TIME		
DIST		
INTENSITY		

Notes :

_____
_____
_____
_____
_____
_____

_____ Date

	CORE BODY	**UPPER BODY**	**LOWER BODY**
EXERCISES			
SETS			
REPS			
WEIGHTS			
REST TIME			

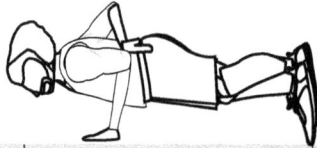

	WARM UP	**COOL DOWN**
ACTIVITY		
SETS		
REPS		
TIME		
DIST		
INTENSITY		

Notes :

_____
_____
_____
_____
_____
_____

_____ Date

	CORE BODY	UPPER BODY	LOWER BODY
EXERCISES			
SETS			
REPS			
WEIGHTS			
REST TIME			

	WARM UP	COOL DOWN
ACTIVITY		
SETS		
REPS		
TIME		
DIST		
INTENSITY		

Notes :

_____
_____
_____
_____
_____
_____

_____ Date

	CORE BODY	UPPER BODY	LOWER BODY
EXERCISES			
SETS			
REPS			
WEIGHTS			
REST TIME			

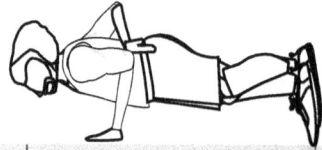

	WARM UP	COOL DOWN
ACTIVITY		
SETS		
REPS		
TIME		
DIST		
INTENSITY		

Notes :
_____
_____
_____
_____
_____
_____

_____ Date

	CORE BODY	UPPER BODY	LOWER BODY
EXERCISES			
SETS			
REPS			
WEIGHTS			
REST TIME			

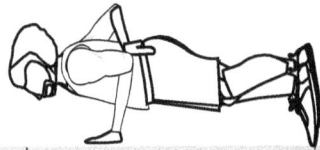

	WARM UP	COOL DOWN
ACTIVITY		
SETS		
REPS		
TIME		
DIST		
INTENSITY		

Notes :

_____
_____
_____
_____
_____
_____

_____ Date

	CORE BODY	UPPER BODY	LOWER BODY
EXERCISES			
SETS			
REPS			
WEIGHTS			
REST TIME			

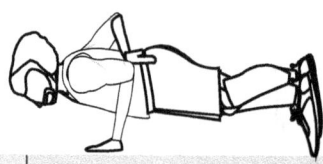

	WARM UP	COOL DOWN
ACTIVITY		
SETS		
REPS		
TIME		
DIST		
INTENSITY		

Notes :

_____
_____
_____
_____
_____
_____

_____ Date

	CORE BODY	UPPER BODY	LOWER BODY
EXERCISES			
SETS			
REPS			
WEIGHTS			
REST TIME			

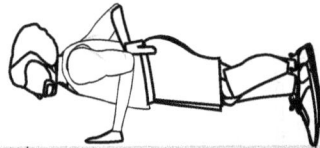

	WARM UP	COOL DOWN
ACTIVITY		
SETS		
REPS		
TIME		
DIST		
INTENSITY		

Notes :
_____
_____
_____
_____
_____
_____

_____ Date

	CORE BODY	**UPPER BODY**	**LOWER BODY**
EXERCISES			
SETS			
REPS			
WEIGHTS			
REST TIME			

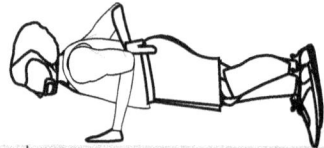

	WARM UP	**COOL DOWN**
ACTIVITY		
SETS		
REPS		
TIME		
DIST		
INTENSITY		

Notes :

_____

_____

_____

_____

_____

_____

_____ Date

	CORE BODY	UPPER BODY	LOWER BODY
EXERCISES			
SETS			
REPS			
WEIGHTS			
REST TIME			

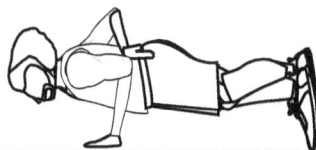

	WARM UP	COOL DOWN
ACTIVITY		
SETS		
REPS		
TIME		
DIST		
INTENSITY		

Notes :

_____
_____
_____
_____
_____
_____

_____ Date

	CORE BODY	UPPER BODY	LOWER BODY
EXERCISES			
SETS			
REPS			
WEIGHTS			
REST TIME			

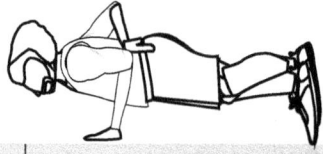

	WARM UP	COOL DOWN
ACTIVITY		
SETS		
REPS		
TIME		
DIST		
INTENSITY		

Notes :

_____
_____
_____
_____
_____
_____

_____ Date

	CORE BODY	UPPER BODY	LOWER BODY
EXERCISES			
SETS			
REPS			
WEIGHTS			
REST TIME			

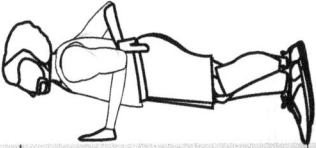

	WARM UP	COOL DOWN
ACTIVITY		
SETS		
REPS		
TIME		
DIST		
INTENSITY		

Notes :

_____
_____
_____
_____
_____
_____

_____ Date

	CORE BODY	**UPPER BODY**	**LOWER BODY**
EXERCISES			
SETS			
REPS			
WEIGHTS			
REST TIME			

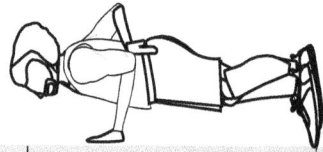

	WARM UP	**COOL DOWN**
ACTIVITY		
SETS		
REPS		
TIME		
DIST		
INTENSITY		

Notes :

_____

_____

_____

_____

_____

_____

_____ Date

	CORE BODY	UPPER BODY	LOWER BODY
EXERCISES			
SETS			
REPS			
WEIGHTS			
REST TIME			

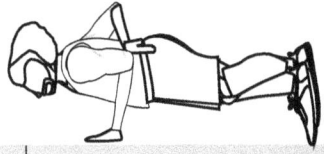

	WARM UP	COOL DOWN
ACTIVITY		
SETS		
REPS		
TIME		
DIST		
INTENSITY		

Notes :
_____
_____
_____
_____
_____
_____

_____ Date

	CORE BODY	UPPER BODY	LOWER BODY
EXERCISES			
SETS			
REPS			
WEIGHTS			
REST TIME			

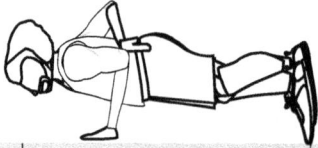

	WARM UP	COOL DOWN
ACTIVITY		
SETS		
REPS		
TIME		
DIST		
INTENSITY		

Notes :
_____
_____
_____
_____
_____
_____

_____ Date

	CORE BODY	UPPER BODY	LOWER BODY
EXERCISES			
SETS			
REPS			
WEIGHTS			
REST TIME			

	WARM UP	COOL DOWN
ACTIVITY		
SETS		
REPS		
TIME		
DIST		
INTENSITY		

Notes :

_____
_____
_____
_____
_____
_____

_____ Date

	CORE BODY	UPPER BODY	LOWER BODY
EXERCISES			
SETS			
REPS			
WEIGHTS			
REST TIME			

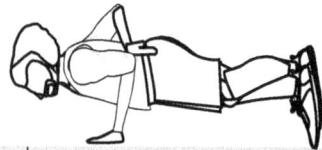

	WARM UP	COOL DOWN
ACTIVITY		
SETS		
REPS		
TIME		
DIST		
INTENSITY		

Notes :
_____
_____
_____
_____
_____
_____

_____ Date

	CORE BODY	UPPER BODY	LOWER BODY
EXERCISES			
SETS			
REPS			
WEIGHTS			
REST TIME			

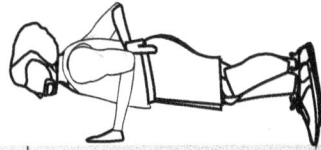

	WARM UP	COOL DOWN
ACTIVITY		
SETS		
REPS		
TIME		
DIST		
INTENSITY		

Notes :

_____
_____
_____
_____
_____
_____

_____ Date

	CORE BODY	UPPER BODY	LOWER BODY
EXERCISES			
SETS			
REPS			
WEIGHTS			
REST TIME			

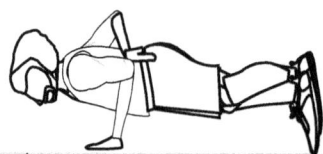

	WARM UP	COOL DOWN
ACTIVITY		
SETS		
REPS		
TIME		
DIST		
INTENSITY		

Notes :

_____
_____
_____
_____
_____
_____

_____ Date

	CORE BODY	UPPER BODY	LOWER BODY
EXERCISES			
SETS			
REPS			
WEIGHTS			
REST TIME			

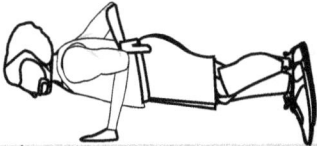

	WARM UP	COOL DOWN
ACTIVITY		
SETS		
REPS		
TIME		
DIST		
INTENSITY		

Notes :
_____
_____
_____
_____
_____
_____

_____ Date

	CORE BODY	UPPER BODY	LOWER BODY
EXERCISES			
SETS			
REPS			
WEIGHTS			
REST TIME			

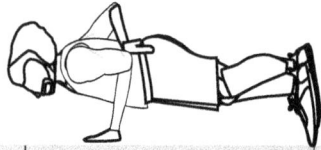

	WARM UP	COOL DOWN
ACTIVITY		
SETS		
REPS		
TIME		
DIST		
INTENSITY		

Notes :
_____
_____
_____
_____
_____
_____

_____ Date

	CORE BODY	UPPER BODY	LOWER BODY
EXERCISES			
SETS			
REPS			
WEIGHTS			
REST TIME			

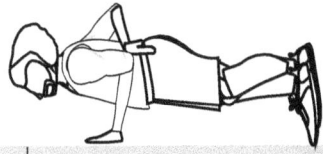

	WARM UP	COOL DOWN
ACTIVITY		
SETS		
REPS		
TIME		
DIST		
INTENSITY		

Notes :

_____
_____
_____
_____
_____
_____

_____ Date

	CORE BODY	**UPPER BODY**	**LOWER BODY**
EXERCISES			
SETS			
REPS			
WEIGHTS			
REST TIME			

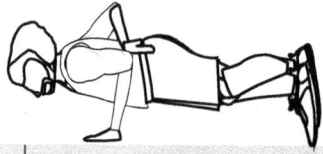

	WARM UP	**COOL DOWN**
ACTIVITY		
SETS		
REPS		
TIME		
DIST		
INTENSITY		

Notes :

_____
_____
_____
_____
_____
_____

_____ Date

	CORE BODY	UPPER BODY	LOWER BODY
EXERCISES			
SETS			
REPS			
WEIGHTS			
REST TIME			

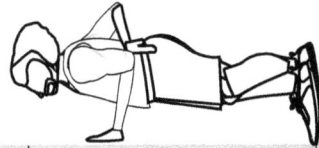

	WARM UP	COOL DOWN
ACTIVITY		
SETS		
REPS		
TIME		
DIST		
INTENSITY		

Notes :

_____
_____
_____
_____
_____
_____

_____ Date

	CORE BODY	UPPER BODY	LOWER BODY
EXERCISES			
SETS			
REPS			
WEIGHTS			
REST TIME			

	WARM UP	COOL DOWN
ACTIVITY		
SETS		
REPS		
TIME		
DIST		
INTENSITY		

Notes :

_____
_____
_____
_____
_____
_____

_____ Date

	CORE BODY	UPPER BODY	LOWER BODY
EXERCISES			
SETS			
REPS			
WEIGHTS			
REST TIME			

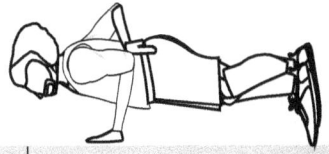

	WARM UP	COOL DOWN
ACTIVITY		
SETS		
REPS		
TIME		
DIST		
INTENSITY		

Notes :

_____
_____
_____
_____
_____
_____

_____ Date

	CORE BODY	**UPPER BODY**	**LOWER BODY**
EXERCISES			
SETS			
REPS			
WEIGHTS			
REST TIME			

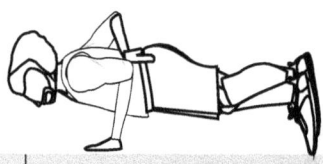

	WARM UP	**COOL DOWN**
ACTIVITY		
SETS		
REPS		
TIME		
DIST		
INTENSITY		

Notes :

_____
_____
_____
_____
_____
_____

_____ Date

	CORE BODY	UPPER BODY	LOWER BODY
EXERCISES			
SETS			
REPS			
WEIGHTS			
REST TIME			

	WARM UP	COOL DOWN
ACTIVITY		
SETS		
REPS		
TIME		
DIST		
INTENSITY		

Notes :
_____
_____
_____
_____
_____
_____

_____ Date

	CORE BODY	**UPPER BODY**	**LOWER BODY**
EXERCISES			
SETS			
REPS			
WEIGHTS			
REST TIME			

	WARM UP	**COOL DOWN**
ACTIVITY		
SETS		
REPS		
TIME		
DIST		
INTENSITY		

Notes :
_____
_____
_____
_____
_____
_____

_____ Date

	CORE BODY	UPPER BODY	LOWER BODY
EXERCISES			
SETS			
REPS			
WEIGHTS			
REST TIME			

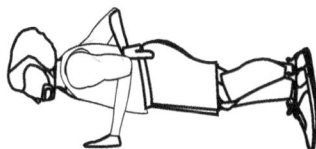

	WARM UP	COOL DOWN
ACTIVITY		
SETS		
REPS		
TIME		
DIST		
INTENSITY		

Notes :

_____

_____

_____

_____

_____

_____

_____ Date

	CORE BODY	UPPER BODY	LOWER BODY
EXERCISES			
SETS			
REPS			
WEIGHTS			
REST TIME			

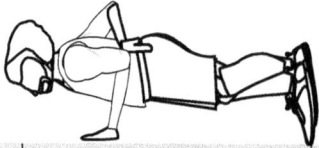

	WARM UP	COOL DOWN
ACTIVITY		
SETS		
REPS		
TIME		
DIST		
INTENSITY		

Notes :

_____
_____
_____
_____
_____
_____

_____ Date

	CORE BODY	UPPER BODY	LOWER BODY
EXERCISES			
SETS			
REPS			
WEIGHTS			
REST TIME			

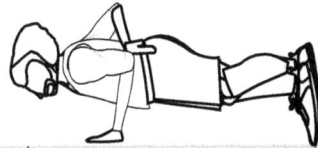

	WARM UP	COOL DOWN
ACTIVITY		
SETS		
REPS		
TIME		
DIST		
INTENSITY		

Notes :

_____
_____
_____
_____
_____
_____

_____ Date

	CORE BODY	UPPER BODY	LOWER BODY
EXERCISES			
SETS			
REPS			
WEIGHTS			
REST TIME			

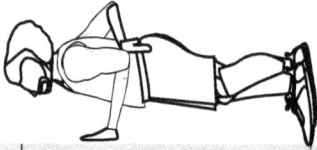

	WARM UP	COOL DOWN
ACTIVITY		
SETS		
REPS		
TIME		
DIST		
INTENSITY		

Notes :

_____
_____
_____
_____
_____
_____

_____ Date

	CORE BODY	UPPER BODY	LOWER BODY
EXERCISES			
SETS			
REPS			
WEIGHTS			
REST TIME			

	WARM UP	COOL DOWN
ACTIVITY		
SETS		
REPS		
TIME		
DIST		
INTENSITY		

Notes :

_____
_____
_____
_____
_____
_____

_____ Date

	CORE BODY	UPPER BODY	LOWER BODY
EXERCISES			
SETS			
REPS			
WEIGHTS			
REST TIME			

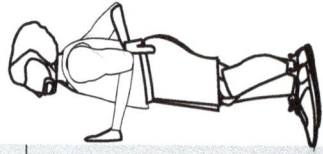

	WARM UP	COOL DOWN
ACTIVITY		
SETS		
REPS		
TIME		
DIST		
INTENSITY		

Notes :
_____
_____
_____
_____
_____
_____

_____ Date

	CORE BODY	UPPER BODY	LOWER BODY
EXERCISES			
SETS			
REPS			
WEIGHTS			
REST TIME			

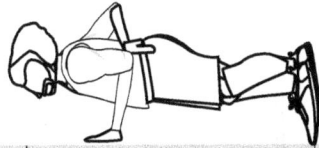

	WARM UP	COOL DOWN
ACTIVITY		
SETS		
REPS		
TIME		
DIST		
INTENSITY		

Notes :

_____

_____

_____

_____

_____

_____

_____ Date

	CORE BODY	UPPER BODY	LOWER BODY
EXERCISES			
SETS			
REPS			
WEIGHTS			
REST TIME			

	WARM UP	COOL DOWN
ACTIVITY		
SETS		
REPS		
TIME		
DIST		
INTENSITY		

Notes :
_____
_____
_____
_____
_____
_____

_____ Date

	CORE BODY	UPPER BODY	LOWER BODY
EXERCISES			
SETS			
REPS			
WEIGHTS			
REST TIME			

	WARM UP	COOL DOWN
ACTIVITY		
SETS		
REPS		
TIME		
DIST		
INTENSITY		

Notes :

_____
_____
_____
_____
_____
_____

_____ Date

	CORE BODY	UPPER BODY	LOWER BODY
EXERCISES			
SETS			
REPS			
WEIGHTS			
REST TIME			

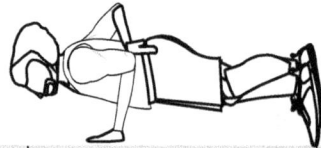

	WARM UP	COOL DOWN
ACTIVITY		
SETS		
REPS		
TIME		
DIST		
INTENSITY		

Notes :

_____
_____
_____
_____
_____
_____

_____ Date

	CORE BODY	UPPER BODY	LOWER BODY
EXERCISES			
SETS			
REPS			
WEIGHTS			
REST TIME			

	WARM UP	COOL DOWN
ACTIVITY		
SETS		
REPS		
TIME		
DIST		
INTENSITY		

Notes :

_____
_____
_____
_____
_____
_____

_____ Date

	CORE BODY	UPPER BODY	LOWER BODY
EXERCISES			
SETS			
REPS			
WEIGHTS			
REST TIME			

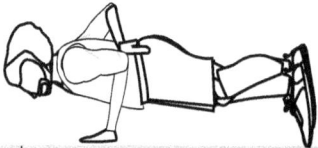

	WARM UP	COOL DOWN
ACTIVITY		
SETS		
REPS		
TIME		
DIST		
INTENSITY		

Notes :
_____
_____
_____
_____
_____
_____

_____ Date

	CORE BODY	**UPPER BODY**	**LOWER BODY**
EXERCISES			
SETS			
REPS			
WEIGHTS			
REST TIME			

	WARM UP	**COOL DOWN**
ACTIVITY		
SETS		
REPS		
TIME		
DIST		
INTENSITY		

Notes :

_____
_____
_____
_____
_____
_____

_____ Date

	CORE BODY	UPPER BODY	LOWER BODY
EXERCISES			
SETS			
REPS			
WEIGHTS			
REST TIME			

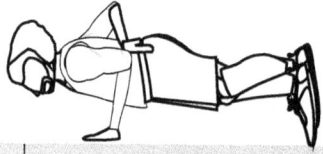

	WARM UP	COOL DOWN
ACTIVITY		
SETS		
REPS		
TIME		
DIST		
INTENSITY		

Notes :

_____
_____
_____
_____
_____
_____

_____ Date

	CORE BODY	UPPER BODY	LOWER BODY
EXERCISES			
SETS			
REPS			
WEIGHTS			
REST TIME			

	WARM UP	COOL DOWN
ACTIVITY		
SETS		
REPS		
TIME		
DIST		
INTENSITY		

Notes :

_____
_____
_____
_____
_____
_____

_____ Date

	CORE BODY	UPPER BODY	LOWER BODY
EXERCISES			
SETS			
REPS			
WEIGHTS			
REST TIME			

	WARM UP	COOL DOWN
ACTIVITY		
SETS		
REPS		
TIME		
DIST		
INTENSITY		

Notes :

_____

_____

_____

_____

_____

_____

_____ Date

	CORE BODY	UPPER BODY	LOWER BODY
EXERCISES			
SETS			
REPS			
WEIGHTS			
REST TIME			

	WARM UP	COOL DOWN
ACTIVITY		
SETS		
REPS		
TIME		
DIST		
INTENSITY		

Notes :

_____
_____
_____
_____
_____
_____

	CORE BODY	UPPER BODY	LOWER BODY
EXERCISES			
SETS			
REPS			
WEIGHTS			
REST TIME			

	WARM UP	COOL DOWN
ACTIVITY		
SETS		
REPS		
TIME		
DIST		
INTENSITY		

Notes :

_____
_____
_____
_____
_____
_____

_____ Date

	CORE BODY	UPPER BODY	LOWER BODY
EXERCISES			
SETS			
REPS			
WEIGHTS			
REST TIME			

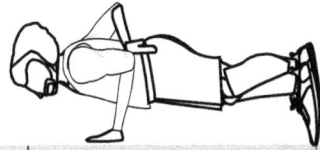

	WARM UP	COOL DOWN
ACTIVITY		
SETS		
REPS		
TIME		
DIST		
INTENSITY		

Notes :

_____
_____
_____
_____
_____
_____

_____ Date

	CORE BODY	UPPER BODY	LOWER BODY
EXERCISES			
SETS			
REPS			
WEIGHTS			
REST TIME			

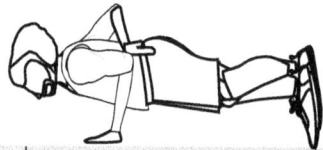

	WARM UP	COOL DOWN
ACTIVITY		
SETS		
REPS		
TIME		
DIST		
INTENSITY		

Notes :
_____
_____
_____
_____
_____
_____

_____ Date

	CORE BODY	UPPER BODY	LOWER BODY
EXERCISES			
SETS			
REPS			
WEIGHTS			
REST TIME			

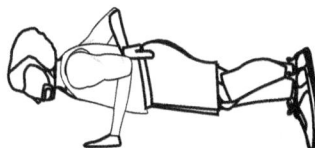

	WARM UP	COOL DOWN
ACTIVITY		
SETS		
REPS		
TIME		
DIST		
INTENSITY		

Notes :

_____
_____
_____
_____
_____
_____

_____ Date

	CORE BODY	**UPPER BODY**	**LOWER BODY**
EXERCISES			
SETS			
REPS			
WEIGHTS			
REST TIME			

	WARM UP	**COOL DOWN**
ACTIVITY		
SETS		
REPS		
TIME		
DIST		
INTENSITY		

Notes :

_____
_____
_____
_____
_____
_____

_____ Date

	CORE BODY	**UPPER BODY**	**LOWER BODY**
EXERCISES			
SETS			
REPS			
WEIGHTS			
REST TIME			

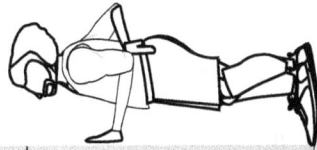

	WARM UP	**COOL DOWN**
ACTIVITY		
SETS		
REPS		
TIME		
DIST		
INTENSITY		

Notes :
_____
_____
_____
_____
_____
_____

_____ Date

	CORE BODY	**UPPER BODY**	**LOWER BODY**
EXERCISES			
SETS			
REPS			
WEIGHTS			
REST TIME			

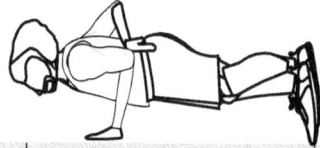

	WARM UP	**COOL DOWN**
ACTIVITY		
SETS		
REPS		
TIME		
DIST		
INTENSITY		

Notes :

_____
_____
_____
_____
_____
_____

_____ Date

	CORE BODY	**UPPER BODY**	**LOWER BODY**
EXERCISES			
SETS			
REPS			
WEIGHTS			
REST TIME			

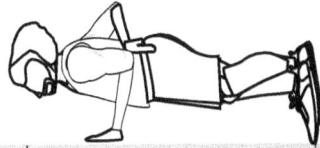

	WARM UP	**COOL DOWN**
ACTIVITY		
SETS		
REPS		
TIME		
DIST		
INTENSITY		

Notes :

_____
_____
_____
_____
_____
_____

_____ Date

	CORE BODY	UPPER BODY	LOWER BODY
EXERCISES			
SETS			
REPS			
WEIGHTS			
REST TIME			

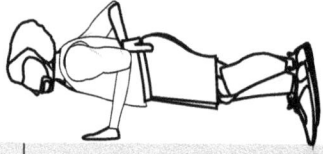

	WARM UP	COOL DOWN
ACTIVITY		
SETS		
REPS		
TIME		
DIST		
INTENSITY		

Notes :
_____
_____
_____
_____
_____
_____

_____ Date

	CORE BODY	**UPPER BODY**	**LOWER BODY**
EXERCISES			
SETS			
REPS			
WEIGHTS			
REST TIME			

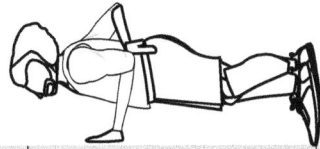

	WARM UP	**COOL DOWN**
ACTIVITY		
SETS		
REPS		
TIME		
DIST		
INTENSITY		

Notes :

_____
_____
_____
_____
_____
_____

www.ingramcontent.com/pod-product-compliance
Lightning Source LLC
Chambersburg PA
CBHW081334090426
42737CB00017B/3139